Rookie
Talk About It™

Conflict Resolution:
When Friends Fight

by Liz George

Content Consultant
Samantha Gambino, Psy.D.
Licensed Psychologist, New York, New York

Reading Consultant
Jeanne M. Clidas, Ph.D.
Reading Specialist

Children's Press®
An Imprint of Scholastic Inc.

Library of Congress Cataloging-in-Publication Data
George, Liz.
  Conflict resolution : when friends fight / by Liz George.
      pages cm. -- (Rookie talk about it)
  Includes index.
  ISBN 978-0-531-21513-5 (library binding) -- ISBN 978-0-531-21381-0 (pbk.) 1. Interpersonal conflict-
-Juvenile literature. 2. Interpersonal conflict in children--Juvenile literature. 3. Friendship--Juvenile
literature. 4. Friendship in children--Juvenile literature. I. Title.

  BF723.I645G46 2016
  303.6'9--dc23   2015018076

Produced by Spooky Cheetah Press
Design by Keith Plechaty

© 2016 by Scholastic Inc.

Printed in China 62

SCHOLASTIC, CHILDREN'S PRESS, ROOKIE TALK ABOUT IT™, and associated logos are trademarks and/or
registered trademarks of Scholastic Inc.

2 3 4 5 6 7 8 9 10 R 25 24 23 22 21 20 19 18 17 16

Photographs ©: cover, 3 top left: Jamie Grill/JGI/Media Bakery; 3 top right: Jupiterimages/Thinkstock;
3 bottom: Susan Chiang/iStockphoto; 4: Visage/Media Bakery; 7 left: glenda/Shutterstock, Inc.; 7
right: michaeljung/Thinkstock; 8: Martin Novak/Thinkstock; 11: Ken Karp Photography; 12: Susan Chiang/
iStockphoto; 15: SolStock/iStockphoto; 16: Paul Bradbury/Media Bakery; 19: David Young-Wolff/PhotoEdit; 20:
Jupiterimages/Thinkstock; 23: Ingram Publishing/Newscom; 24: Jamie Grill/JGI/Media Bakery; 26: Howard
Sochurek/The LIFE Picture Collection/Getty Images; 27: Robert W. Kelley/The LIFE Picture Collection/Getty
Images; 28: Absodels/Getty Images; 29: Canaryluc/Shutterstock, Inc.; 30: Stockchildren/Alamy Images;
31 top: Paul Bradbury/Media Bakery; 31 center top: Martin Novak/Thinkstock; 31 center bottom: karens4/
Thinkstock; 31 bottom: Absodels/Getty Images.

Table of Contents

What Is Conflict?

Your friend comes to your house to play. You want to ride bikes outside. He wants to stay inside and play video games. You think it is your turn to choose. This is a **conflict**.

A conflict happens when you disagree strongly with someone and it is hard to reach a solution. Conflict **resolution** means you both try to understand each other better. You work to find a solution.

Not every disagreement is a conflict. You think basketball is the best sport. Your friend says baseball is better. In this case, it is okay to agree to disagree!

Friendships Come with Conflict

Everyone fights. Sometimes it is easy to make up. Other times hurt feelings get in the way. Conflict can make you feel angry, sad, or confused. Your friend might be having those feelings, too.

Here are some ways to resolve conflicts:

- Stay calm. This will make it easier to find a solution.

- Try to **compromise**. Find a solution you can both agree on.

- Ask for what you need. Then really listen to your friend. Try to understand what he needs.

- Use "I-statements." Do not say "*You* hurt my feelings." Say "*I* felt upset." Your friend will know how you feel, and he will not feel attacked.

Believe it or not, conflicts are an important part of friendships. When you find a way to be friends again after a conflict, your friendship is stronger because you worked together.

Read about the problems some friends have faced. Maybe their stories can help you when you have a conflict.

Working It Out

Luis tripped Rodney during their soccer game. Now Rodney is angry. He wants to shout at his friend. Instead, he takes a deep breath. He closes his eyes and slowly counts to 10. Now that he is calm, Rodney is ready to talk to Luis about why he is angry.

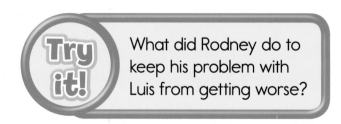

Try it!

What did Rodney do to keep his problem with Luis from getting worse?

Madison and Caleb both want to hold the class pet. They cannot agree on who should go first. "Let's compromise," says Madison. "We can flip a coin to see who holds the bird first."

Try it!

Was flipping a coin a good way to find a solution?

Lily thinks Zoe was being mean during art. So Lily decides to ignore her for the rest of the day. Now Zoe's feelings are hurt. She asks Lily what happened. She listens as Lily explains. Then she tells her side of the story. "I was working on my project and did not think I would have time to finish," she says. "I was not trying to be mean."

Each girl begins to understand how the other feels. They are friends again.

Try it!

What helped Lily and Zoe become friends again?

19

Abby and Charlotte have always been best friends. Lately, Charlotte has been spending a lot of time with Taylor. Abby is feeling jealous.

After school, she decides to tell Charlotte what is bothering her. She says, "I am worried that Taylor is your new best friend." Charlotte says, "I have a lot of friends, but no one will ever take your place!" Abby is happy she shared her feelings.

We Can Cooperate

Sometimes you might need to ask a grown-up to help settle a conflict. If you and your friend cannot agree, ask someone else to listen to both sides. That person can help you find a solution.

Conflict resolution happens with **cooperation**. You and your friend must work together to solve a problem. You also need to compromise. That means you both understand that you might get some of what you want. But you will not get everything you want.

When friends learn how to resolve conflicts, everyone feels better!

Try it!

The next time you have a conflict, think of two things you could do to resolve it. Ask your friend to do the same. Choose a solution together.

Martin Luther King Jr.

Martin Luther King Jr. showed people how to resolve conflicts without violence.

Martin Luther King Jr. was born in Altanta, Georgia, on January 15, 1929. During his lifetime, African-American people faced unfair treatment in many places in the United States.

Laws in Southern states kept black people from holding certain jobs. They were also kept separate from white people. For example, black people had to eat in different restaurants, go to different schools, and use separate restrooms from white people. The things that were meant for African-American people were never as good as those that white people used.

King was tired of the unfair treatment. He wanted to change the way black people were treated in America. He became a leader of the Civil Rights Movement—the fight to give black people the same rights and freedoms white people have.

People believed in King. They trusted him. When he said they had to work to find a peaceful solution to unfair laws, people followed him. King led marches so people would understand the problems black people faced. Through his work, King was able to bring about change. He is one of America's greatest heroes.

It Starts with You!

Become a peacemaker. Here's how:

1. Use chance to solve conflict. Flip a coin. Roll dice. Play rock, paper, scissors. These are all are easy ways to settle a conflict, like who gets to go first when playing a game.

2. Apologize. Imagine you accidentally bump into a friend or do something to hurt his or her feelings. Sometimes just saying "I am sorry" can make conflict disappear.

3. Act it out. Grab two stuffed animals or a pair of puppets and act out a conflict with a friend. Show your friend how you felt.

What Would You Do?

Read the story below and imagine what you might do in this situation.

Your mom says you can ask one friend to go to the movies on Saturday. You ask your friend Danielle to come. Later, your friend Mia comes to you and says she is angry that you did not ask her to go to the movies. Now you do not know what to do.

Need help getting started?

- What should you say to Mia to help her understand your decision?

- Is there someone you can ask for advice?

How Do You Handle Conflict?

1. When you are angry at someone, you

   A. yell.

   B. walk away.

   C. tell them why.

2. When it comes to solving problems, it is important to

   A. win the argument.

   B. say everything you want to say.

   C. listen as well as talk.

3. To resolve a conflict, you

   A. move on and forget about it.

   B. talk about only what actually happened.

   C. talk about what might help you both feel better.

Answer key: A: 1 point, B: 2 points, C: 3 points

If you scored 6-9 points, you are able to deal with conflict and find solutions. If you scored 3-5 points, conflict will be easier if you try to talk and listen more to others and share your feelings, too.

Glossary

compromise (KOM-pruh-mize): when each person gives up something in order to get along

conflict (KAHN-flikt): a disagreement with someone that gets in the way of your friendship

cooperation (koh-OP-uh-ray-shun): the act of working together to get something done

resolution (rez-uh-LOO-shun): solution to a conflict or problem

Index

Facts for Now

Visit this Scholastic Web site for more information on conflict resolution:
www.factsfornow.scholastic.com
Enter the keywords **Conflict Resolution**

About the Author

Liz George is a writer and a licensed psychotherapist. She lives in Montclair, New Jersey, with her husband, Rob, her son, Zack, and her daughter, Ava. Liz enjoys helping teenagers get in touch with their feelings.